Hemispheres

HEMISPHERES

Poems by Grace Schulman

The Sheep Meadow Press
New York

©1984 by Grace Schulman. All rights reserved. Published 1984

Typesetting by Keystrokes, Lenox, Mass.
Printed in the United States of America

The Sheep Meadow Press, New York, N.Y.

Distributed by Persea Books
225 Lafayette Street, New York, N.Y. 10012

Library of Congress Cataloging in Publication Data

Schulman, Grace.
    Hemispheres.

    I. Title.
PS3569.C538H4   1984   811'.54   84-14055
ISBN 0-935296-55-7
ISBN 0-935296-56-5 (pbk)

ACKNOWLEDGMENTS

I am grateful to the editors of magazines in which the following poems first appeared:

American Poetry Review: *Sutton Hoo Ship Burial.*
Antaeus: *The Messenger.*
Crosscurrents: *Songs of Our Cells* (published as *Waking to Song*).
Forthcoming: *Correspondence, Instructions for a Journey.*
The Georgia Review: *Freedom Fighter* (published as *Adultery*), *Losses.*
Glyph: *Letter from Nicaragua.*
The Gramercy Review: *Villanelle.*
Grand Street: *Division, Echocardiogram, The Flight, Par Avion, Trompe L'Oeil.*
The Hudson Review: *The Stars and the Moon.*
The Nation: *Burning the Dead, Hemispheres.*
The New Yorker: *Easy as Wind.*
The Ontario Review: *Dawn Over the East River, The Swans.*
Poetry: *Blessed is the Light, Flight Commands, New Year, Port of Many Names.*
Present Tense: *Jerusalem Street Talk, Waiting Music.*
Shenandoah: *"Let There Be Translators!," The Marsh.*
The Yale Review: *City of Many Names.*

"Easy as Wind" and "Blessed is the Light" were reprinted in *The Pearl* (Copenhagen, Denmark). "Letter from Nicaragua" appeared in a sequence entitled "Four Days of Summer," in *El Pez y la Serpiente* (Managua, Nicaragua), translated into Spanish by Mario Cajina-Vega. "The Source" appeared in *New Macedonia* (Scopje, Yugoslavia), translated into Macedonian by Meto Jovanovski.

With gratitude to
The Corporation of Yaddo
The Macdowell Colony
The Michael Karolyi Memorial Foundation
and
The Mishkenot Sha'ananim
where many of these poems were written

In memory of my father,
Bernard Waldman

*"Console toi, tu ne me chercherais pas,
si tu ne m'avais pas trouvé."*

*"Be comforted: you would not search for me
if you had not found me."*

Pascal,
Pensées

*"The sea is the color of the sky:
they are two seas bound together.
Between them, my heart is a third sea,
as my praise soars in new waves."*

Judah Halevi,
"The Poet Imagines His Voyage"

CONTENTS

I. BLESSED IS THE LIGHT

II. HEMISPHERES

III. FLIGHT COMMANDS

IV. SEACOASTS OF THREE CONTINENTS

V. INSTRUCTIONS FOR A JOURNEY

I. BLESSED IS THE LIGHT

BLESSED IS THE LIGHT

Blessed is the light that turns to fire, and blessed the flames
    that fire makes of what it burns.
Blessed the inexhaustible sun, for it feeds the moon that shines
    but does not burn.
Praised be hot vapors in earth's crust, for they force up
    mountains that explode as molten rock and cool, like
    love remembered.
Holy is the sun that strikes sea, for surely as water burns
    life and death are one. Holy the sun, maker of change, for
    it melts ice into water that bruises mountains, honing peaks
    and carving gullies.
Sacred is the mountain that grows compact, less porous, over
    time. Jagged peaks promise permanence but change, planed
    by rockslides, cut by avalanche, crushed, eroded, leached
    of minerals.
Sacred the rock that spins for centuries before it shines,
    governed by gravity, burning into sight near earth's orbit,
    for it rises falling, surviving night.
Behold the arcs your eyes make when you speak. Behold the
    hands, white fire. Branches of pine, holding votive candles, they
    command, disturbed by wind, the fire that sings in me.
Blessed is whatever alters, turns, revolves, just as the gods
    move when the mind moves them.
Praised be the body, our bodies, that lie down and open and rise,
    falling in flame.

CITY OF MANY NAMES

Jerusalem, meaning "holy," is unholy.
The morning sun strikes stone walls bone and amber,
turns a black cone ochreous at noon
and cuts new shadows slate-gray, olive-green.
A gold and a silver cupola seem stationary,
but change like the sun and moon: The Dome of the Rock
swells and inflames Al-Aqsa. Nothing is stable.

Jerusalem, meaning "whole," has been divided
by roads, lines, streets that alter with each war.
The Old City's in quarters behind battlements.
The cannon shot of Ramadan explodes
above the Western Wall, where men and women
whisper to what's unseen behind the wall.

Loudspeakers blare muezzin chants and drown
church bells, sabbath prayers. The local music:
shellbursts, sonic booms and people's voices,
clear as birds. Unfounded city. Fallen,
everything rises: Mary flies to heaven;
Mohammed gallops skyward on a horse;
flames curl to many gods. In this dark chapel,
the Copts intone and, nearby, Ethiopians
sing praises, while a man rests on his hands
and knees, face to the ground, under black icons.

Borders that terrify have summoned me
to cancel edges, nullify horizons;
mirrors of my mind transform divisions.
I climbed a winding road and discovered seas
in air; waves silver hills, their cadences
winds seething through trees, partitions gone.
It was a miracle, or an illusion:
When I walked down, the boundaries reappeared.

Yet cypresses that vanish are still there.
At night this soldier's name cut in white stone
is gone; salamanders with snowflake feet
turn soap-colored and orange on the terrace.
Even the stone walls waver behind acacias.
Jerusalem has shadows that recede
in spangling sun as tide effaces seamarks.
I live for what I never have believed.

"LET THERE BE TRANSLATORS!"

"And the Lord said, 'Behold, the people is one and they have all one language...Go to, let us go down, and there confuse their language, that they may not understand one another's speech.'"

Genesis xi: 6, 7.

When God confused our languages, he uttered,
in sapphire tones: "Let there be translators!"
And there were conjurors and necromancers
and alchemists, but they did not suffice:
they turned trees into emeralds, pools to seas.

God spoke again: "Let there be carpenters
who fasten edges, caulk the seams, splice timbers."
They were good.
                    God said: "Blessed the builder
who leaves his tower, turns from bricks and mortar
to marvel at the flames, the smith who fumbles
for prongs, wields andirons and prods live coals,
who stokes the hearth and welds two irons as one."

Praised was the man who wrote his name in other
handwriting, who spoke in other tones,
who, knowing elms, imagined ceiba trees
and cypresses as though they were his own,
finding new music in each limitation.

Holy the one who lost his speech to others,
subdued his pen, resigned his failing sight
to change through fire's change, until he saw
earth's own fire, the radiant rock of words.

SUTTON HOO SHIP BURIAL

*(In the British Museum are glass cases filled with objects belonging to a
7th century Anglo-Saxon king, and found in the remains of a large
boat in August, 1939, at Sutton Hoo, on Suffolk's River Deben, near
the North Sea.)*

He rose out of the sea, the last warrior,
months before Dunkirk, days before invasion,
not his remains, but things: a boar's-head brooch;
epaulets, coins; a six-stringed willow harp;
christening spoons beside an auroch's horn.
His helmet found, the absent king endured,
his house battered by water; and however
fire forced up his praise, he was born in water.

As water changes into ice and fog
and kills, it broke the hull, scattering timbers
until the narrow strakes were marks in the sand,
nail prints; but the hull would give life back again
as snails plunge into earth before the spring—
a resurrection shell; so he appeared,
beached among swampferns fronded in the bog,
monarch of nests and ruler of enclosures.

He may have been the real Beowulf,
bee-keeper, guardian of law. He fought nightmares,
not men: he conquered trolls and firedragons
and slew Cain's sons, sea-monsters, keeping peace
within himself, knowing the heart's Grendels
that brought invaders, past and future wars.
The country waned, lacking that curious hero,
for Danelaw split the kingdom, killing men.

Weeks before lightning war, and the sea blockades,
men found the bark of the last warrior
who ruled alone. It was a cenotaph:
his body lay in heath covered with bracken.
A pagan ship, a Christian burial
in holy ground for a king who sanctified
God and the gods. Not his remains but things
would sail him to the next world as a king.

Ring-giver, father of swords, of artisans,
emerging, moving towards me in the night,
he brings me dreams of refuge in a shell,
conchologist of the imagination.
I see his shadow now, for I hear my past
in my body's shell, in reveries of almonds.
As he loomed out of the sea to tell his story
of mud-drenched creatures in the mind's black waters

who thrashed ungoverned ghosts at the sea's edge,
I find my house in a stone, my world in acorns,
my solitude in galleys holding bowls,
bronze stags, gold buckles, swords inlaid with garnets,
stars locked in hollows, hidden and revealed,
invisible, asleep, burning to live.
In rocks I will know eels and sea-anemones
before I surface into murderous air.

ECHOCARDIOGRAM

Flashed on a radar screen in serpentine
sonar waves, the heart is not a Valentine,
nor a candy box, nor visceral, nor red.
Sea breakers crest and fall, wash in, recede.

Wash in, recede. My heart moves linden trees,
thrums with the squall of jays, the cries of towhees.

"These are the chambers of your heart," he drawled.
"This, the aortic action. Here's the valve:
Mitral valve prolapse, echo positive.
Be comforted. It means nothing at all."

Nothing at all. The heart winces and stirs,
blazes at miracles, battens on fear.

The source of palpitations, found at last
by a black machine, strapped to the knees and chest,
that captures the echo of the heart, refines
its booming energy in sinuous lines.

Sinuous lines, at least. That seaweed green
rapture that thuds and drums and beats like rain.

"We can control your rapid beats," he droned,
without a fault or fissure. I had seen,
under the ocean waves, on a smaller frame,
green fire leap to the heart's brass kettledrums.

Brass kettledrums. Echocardiogram,
nymph invisible but for a song,
restore me now, but why does the heart grow numb
to the rock-faced man who died alone, despairing?

Radar angel, what of the hawk's sway,
the bulrush, marigolds, the heron's cry,
of earth's erratic lights and shadows? There
let your needle calculate disorder.

THE BENEDICTION

Forgetting even that he had forgotten,
burning with silence, eyes gone gray, his face
suddenly corroded, sea-beaten rock,
he spoke: "My father punished or commanded
only, but on the Eve of Rosh Hashana,
he cupped our faces, one by one, and kissed us."
Then as we stood, he hefted bony shoulders,
hauled up skeleton hands and trembling feet,
clutched a bedside table, cleared the sea
out of his throat and chanted in two languages:
"May the Lord bless you and keep you. May he make
his face to shine upon you, and be gracious."

THE REAL LOSS

You are the real loss:
not the man who spoke like you,
not strangers' passing hands,
but your sea-green eyes that widened
when you saw yellow glass bottles
in Cartier's windows.

Too quick to check
your ungoverned stride
for anyone, you resigned your life
to the thin shadow
that knifed your doorway.

The waves wash out, then leave
shallow green water,
the marble of your veins,
the prints of your arteries.

The wind tries
your five languages
all at once,

and cloud-shapes alter
just as you refused
not to change.

The gull floats sunward;
the sea resumes its railing course;
the full moon
whitens your face,
unformed and recast
each passing day.

SONGS OF MY FATHERS

(Schmuel, my grandmother's grandfather, came from Romania with the Homestead Act of 1862 to Garden City, Kansas, where he sold steam tractors and farm machines.)

Sliding a skull-cap under a wide-brimmed hat,
you wore a Star of David and a sheriff's badge,
had sideburns and a beard, and carried guns.
Even in those fields you guarded law,
David before the Ark, shouting thanksgiving
for flaming words whose shadows made men tremble.

Your sons went East to marry in the faith
and all returned except my ancestor,
Zavel, who fathered caretakers of synagogues,
then resolute cantors; later, baritone lawyers.

I studied yellowed books in cloistered rooms
to find you, then I searched that woman's eyes,
her voice a battering wind. "What of the faith?"
I asked my grandmother, who closed her book,
The Range of Reason. "It is tenacity,"
she said. "The will to live, to sing, to change."

To sing. To chant. To change: cantors, *cantare*.
They were enchanted, turning song to fire.

I wonder, though, of others who remained,
farmers in Oregon and South Dakota,
dancing to laws that regulate their acts.
Their flames rise up on Friday nights; they leave
chairs vacant, never dreaming of Elijah.

Sometimes they drink wine from silver cups,
singing like sea-wind, savage joy and pain
grown into thunder. They never question
why, from where, that perilous song has come.

THE SOURCE

Not like the murky city waters,
gunmetal at dawn, the River Drim,
limpid as pure recall, flows from Lake Ohrid,
itself unbruised, displaying
islands of phragmites
and curly pungweed growing from the floor
like memories surfacing. Tracing the river
to its source, as though I'd find
sulfurous thoughts at mind's end like the stars
at the bottom of Dante's hell, like sallow ghosts
grown into ringing brightnesses, I sailed
to a granite island, and saw
near an abandoned monastery,
where peacocks flourish in walnut trees,
a spring swell into Lake Ohrid, which,
damned to break its flow, surges
into the village of Struga, between banks
of poplars with pointillist leaves,
hauling boys who dive for coins.

One evening, quicksilver at moonrise,
the river carried voices
choiring against the current.
The source was song.

II. HEMISPHERES

HEMISPHERES

Our bodies, luminary under bedclothes,
fit tightly like the pieces of a broken
terra cotta vase that is newly mended,
smooth surfaces, no jagged edges visible.

I've read that countries were so interlocked
before the oceans fractured them and splayed
Mexico enfolding Mauritania;
Brazil's round shoulder hoisted to Nigeria;
Italy pressing Libya; Alaska
so linked with Russia in the Bering Straits
that fingers touched, like dead hands on a harp.
Our tremulous hands held fast in sleep at dawn;
legs, arms entwined, one continent, one mass.

EASY AS WIND

Easy as wind that lifts white pine
and blows for flowers, showering rose
petals on cold marble statues,
we touch and separate.
                        I am familiar
with water burning the land,
turning catbrier to red-brown wire,
clinging to live. I have seen flame
waiting to burn, altering shadows,
striking rectangles beyond the trees.
Even the sea collects its powers and strikes,
baffling the sand's composure.
                              But now, suddenly,
wherever I look I see wind
I cannot see, touching nowhere, everywhere.

MORNING SONG

Norwegian spruce trees, veering to red-brown.
You are asleep, your body cool as dawn.
As I turn to leave, sun strikes the terrace,
affirming day. Amazed, through junipers,
my eyes raise watchmen on the mansion tower.
Our clothes will spin together in the laundromat:
doomed lovers circle, drifting on the winds.

VILLANELLE

Moving on the minutes of each other
we join and turn away, and utter praise
that all life changes: earth, rock, fire, water.

At dawn we watch the wind lift junipers,
push clouds, bring weather, turn the sea to spray;
we move on the minutes of each other,

naked, seeing the morning light that alters
shadows, charge, ignite in sudden blaze
and know life changes: earth, rock, fire, water.

As water moves through mountains, falls in vapor
our eyes are clock-hands, measuring the ways
we move on the minutes of each other.

Mornings part us; waking in pines together
we lose our wholeness to acclaim our days
of life that changes: earth, rock, fire, water.

Have me in luminous reveries, and never
in stasis. Fire feeds as it destroys.
Moving on the minutes of each other
we are the life that changes earth, rock, fire, water.

THE SWANS

All day I have thought of the swans
that flew skyward, bellowing,
maundering at first,
immense and web-footed,
fanning tousled wings,
parting the stream
then surging through air.
I know you will pass and return,
your body tense, then writhing,
undulant, coiled in sleep,
your silver eyes mirroring my eyes,
your hands raveled and free,
that somewhere the swans have alighted
on lucent water,
their spiral forms
utterly denying
turbulent flight.

LOSSES

Life's gains are losses: water leaches rock,
rivers erode and deltas restore the land;
the sun melts ice, turns rain to clouds of mist.
Wind that spins palms in circles like propellers
squanders its force; the fire that feeds destroys.

Each morning burns what night had bound together,
waking us, amazed, staring in wonder
that bodies riveted could break apart
to forget wholeness and regain the light.
So for all things neglected, failed, refused,
I turn, as ships spill wind to change their course:
Just as the sea recedes, I grow with loss.

THE STARS AND THE MOON

(In The Legends of the Jews, *Louis Ginzberg writes that an Egyptian princess hung a tapestry woven with diamonds and pearls above King Solomon's bed. When the king wanted to rise, he thought he saw stars and, believing it was night, slept on.)*

Scaling ladders with buckets of white enamel,
I painted the stars and the moon on my window panes
to hold back days and nights. I yanked the telephone,
and stopped the wooden clock. The weeks a lightning-stroke,
desire turned into love. With my blue diamond,
I sliced minutes in half and made days vanish,
fooling the hours.

               I became so skillful
at firmaments that miracles occurred:
a bearded comet moved across the room
breeding no omens, tearing no major kingdoms
into small provinces, but there it was,
reminding us that rock may spin and flare,
lifting the senses, burning into sight.

You eased pale hands away; I saw your shoulders
recede through doorways, watched your image fail
with your famished smile. I left our room
with dream-filled eyes and, standing in the sun,
I gazed at bricks and glass and saw, suddenly,
flashing in stony light, the stars and the moon.

THE MESSENGER

I would have been surprised, but I had seen him
halting at daybreak, hovering around,
ploughing a sky half-dark with stars, half-mauve
with iridescent clouds, then watched him circle,
flutter and glide through buckled window panes.

"I am a superior Hebrew angel," he announced.
"I have one thousand eyes and many wings."
"Don't give me angels," I said, seeing the cherub
plummet, shout his praise and rearrange
layers of wings, then suddenly ignite.
And as I listened, I glanced at your chair,
saw how the bed assumed your body's form,
recalled how mouth-on-mouth we slept, and how
your hands were lightning spears.
                                    You went away.
How could I know that I would sign my name
as yours, that I would hear your words
as miracles, and question other vows
for your laws, written in white fire.

It was that Hebrew angel, made of air
and wind, who caused it all.
He seized my vision, chanted in your voice,
and still stands vigil, writing what I say
in monolithic letters in a register
of pale blue linen. Beyond the angel,
sun that never brightens, never fades.

BORDERS

I

Hemispheres merge. Blinded by margins, cables,
I'd enter circles, shoulder through enclosures.
My body moves through seething waves, dissolving
in incandescent spray. I'd walk through valleys
containing mountains that recede before me.

II

I remember a forbidden line—
a meteor flashing though a paved black road
I was never to cross alone. Low to the ground,
at six, I faced an ocean with a visible
meridian. Far off lived Grace, my namesake:
dear lemon-yellow friend, with agate eyes,
sun-spangled hair more radiant than mine;
phosphemes, angles of light, danced when she shone,
hugging the trees we named, and I heard her laughter
like a stone someone has skipped across the water
of another shore. On her neck an argent saint
burned like a scar. One day I crossed the line
to cut chalk rectangles we stepped inside.
Her mother signaled, washed us clean as brides
to see the church. Hands parted us. I knew
the marker's danger was that place where sand
abraded those graved letters of my fathers'
stone tablets, charms that banished other worlds.

III

Israel: Once a wall of fire beckoned me;
guns volleyed after dark, the morning lull
broken by rain-chants. Then I passed the cypress,
doum palm and eucalyptus, leaving green land.
Men in caftans gave me water there.
Beloved enemies, we watched day's light
fade lines. Suddenly faltering, I whispered,
"Where is the frontier?" looking behind me.
They said: "Our border moves. It is where you are.
Wherever you are standing, it will be."

IV

Vence

Divisions reappear in this fissured valley.
The river that sings through rock cannot be seen.
Above us, limestone terraces are walls,
and shadows have no boundaries after nightfall.
Recall those colors and scars dividing nations
on schoolroom maps and now, partitions gone,
see cobalt streams, chrome deserts, sapphire hills.
And you, love, with your bedlam of Slavic sounds,
Cyrillic alphabet of cave inscriptions,
are man and woman, neither and the same.
Sun's fire transforms, conjoins. I've moved again
to a land of wind-slapped rocks and dangerous eddies;
no safety zones, no lanes, and never borders.

III. FLIGHT COMMANDS

WHAT WE CALL COURAGE

You say the ocean's spray rises
and soaks the redwoods on the mountain
beyond your home, and has for centuries,
and you are right: the patient, long
marriage of many years is what we call
courage, and it is good
to make love new each day
just as the sun rises,
and find yourself instilled
in your wife as you hear music
flow through your bodies.

How, then, shall I speak of our love
that may crash itself out in foam,
that turns a telephone into a black flower
when your voice rushes through it,
across continents, over trees, under oceans.
An angel of silence dies
when we recite the holy litany
of "love" we have unlocked
in each others' throats,
and although telephone words,
they say, are never actual,
when we meet there has been no parting.

Truly, our love is unlawful;
when you arrive at airports,
your face tightens
as though you were smuggling grenades,
but once we are alone
there is no distance between us,

and there is distance everywhere;
griefs dissolve
in the air we travel.

My body was made for the joy
we give each other at the same moment;
our harsh, unmusical cries are death-rattles
acclaiming day; the life-blood courses through us,
our minds quicker because our bodies
contain one another.

Last night, you wrote, you saw *Camille* again,
and would have cried if you had been alone,
and I guessed at what you meant by "alone,"
and you wrote that your valley is gray
because we are not together,

and I see the newsreel footage
of our lives:

how we have walked to bed
in one long sinuous motion,
how we have babbled about the Mabinogion
even as we made love,
and fallen into silences,
how, at dinner with friends,
we lowered our eyes as they collided,
and tried to deflect compass needles
from their true courses.

And I ask myself if leaving you
would be what we call courage
and, for want of an answer,
I resolve never to let go,

for even when you are
halfway across the world,
you are here
on the altering green lawn;
the red-veined maple leaves
call back your hands,
the silver hills
your shoulders and hips
as you lie on your side.

I know that our loves
have honorific models:
Tristan and Isolde met once a year
under a sword; Dante only saw
Beatrice. I may be the Laura
Petrarch never touched, or the Olympia
whose winding device Hoffmann blurred
through tinted glasses.

I peer through a leaf-shaped sky
and see not you but another,
his face etched in a juniper,

"Man in a Yellow Coat"
in the Jeu de Paume, where light
pours rectangles on the floor,
Van Gogh's chrome pursuing me,
and I hear in your voice
no angel's rhythm
but an angel's melody,
because in eternity
there is no time
but there is
praise.

NOTES FROM UNDERGROUND

Your voice strides over mountains, flows through veined
waterways: "I cannot leave. I can."
Trapped in a plastic cube, in hand-to-hand
combat with yourself, you watch the telephone
dissolve in blood. You have another love;
you speak to her in durable sounds, to me
in songs others can't hear: the clamor of leaves,
the drumming of death-watch beetles.
                                    Yesterday,
volcanic dust rained in for thousands of miles,
goring the sunset, and electrified
the sky's vermilion. Harmonic tremors came,
and tore open my eyes, although for once
I was content, asleep, in other arms.
Magma raised deadly clouds, forced up my voice
that called out one word only, the word: your name.

FLIGHT COMMANDS

All seat backs must be upright. For your safety
no smoking during take-off.
                              (How you arched
your back, wet from the shower, a whale rising,
then crushed a cigarette, and phoned for whiskey.
Outside our double room, birds vaulted wires
on Route 9A; beyond, your mountain home.)

Should you need oxygen ...
                              (Hands covered my face;
you whispered, mouth-to-mouth, then stammered, wordless;
your lips opened and closed without a sound,
your chest contracting when you freed my hand.)

Emergency doors appear on either side
of cabins.
          (Our emergency is permanent:
no exit, no "Way Out." Three thousand miles,
six hours apart, we travestied our names,
and ambushed twenty hours. Still ascending,
we never have reached stable altitudes.)

Seat cushions are flotation aids.
                              (We floated
on an Aegean of the mind, heard wind
soughing in what had been an air conditioner,
then heard it hum, mechanical again.)

There is a chance of turbulence.
                              (In clouds,
your face with trenched lines, blurs, then utters flame.)

We're passing *Sage, The Great Divide, St. Cloud,*
Lake Michigan . . .
                         (The Mare Serenitatis.
There's Tebel just ahead, where double people
shout at themselves, a land of emerald light.
The fire I see flickering from the wing
is firmament parting a new heaven and earth. . . .

When you drew near I dreamed I was a letter
imploring God to make the world through me.
Now I have rooted deep inside your sentences.
I hear the behemoth roar, the ziz cry out.
I walk the five worlds God destroyed, observe
caves with black scorpions, fire-gold salamanders.)

We wait for clearance.

                         (There may never be
clearance, but this clearness fills my hours.
Fog shrouds the aircraft, but on facing sides
the sun ignites the sea, the moon rises.
Above us, sulfurous angels praise
a new beginning. I have looked down and seen
tentative amber lights that blink and fade,
radiant worlds emerge, dissolve and change.
The fog lifts. I have heard your voice.)

NEW YEAR

Eight thousand miles, twelve hours from home. I came
to stare at jasmine in blue Hebron glass,
a terra cotta lamp, a lacquered table,
a carved oak chest with surplus drawers and hangers.

Outside the window, cargo boats were scattered.
They had moved soundlessly at night, but blared
salutes to my Gregorian New Year.
One ancient stone arm jutted into sea,
a golden breakwater. After you reckoned
the birthdays, solstices and holy days
gone by since we had met, you spoke in sleep
in several languages. You uttered: "Neuf.
It's a French dream." "Je t'adore," I answered.
"Correct," you said, your arm a promontory.

A yellow land bird shook the outsize window.
Still unafraid of other hands between us,
ready to part, we stiffened on the highway,
driving to the airport into sunrise.
"Close your eyes," you warned. "The sun's first rays
will blind you." Chilled, I looked. Our dawn.

FREEDOM FIGHTER

Unarmed, you guarded seven craggy hills
of a city, watching for hands that hurled
grenades. Ordered to freeze,
you disobeyed commands, and moved
down sandstone cliffs
and pine forests,
tearing your sleeves on brambles,
hiding in trenches.

Clear-sighted still,
with bifocals, respected now,
you guard your hidden love.
Your wife's the tyrant you have glued together,
a Wizard of Oz you run with belts and ratchets,
protector-dictator who governs you,
leader who has not threatened to assassinate,
or even apprehend.
Neighbors are the soldiers who outnumber you,
your friends your enemies.

Your city's safe, but not the secret name
of one you move toward. Even in peace
a night marauder,
you touch her arm and say,
"I have never felt so free,"
hounded on rocks,
trekking through sand,
wading through dangerous eddies,
startled when birds
twitter in groves
and some small thing
rattles thickets.

WAITING MUSIC

The pomegranate swings
from a spindly branch
like a temple bell;
bronze now,
it reddens in the sun.
At night,
outside the chancel window,
a quarter moon grows,
lifts the stricken
battlemented wall
and startles trees.
Wind sends leaves plummeting
to the dark valley.
Blue and white flowers
vanish and are there.
I know you will return
when the moon is full.

PAR AVION

I peeled the aerogram and freed his voice:
"My only love, the air is dense
with sand; the world is gray
in this brief autumn. Your words
are talismans. I am here and gone,
for nothing fixes you as love does,
or wrenches you away so violently.
My body starves without you
like the waning moon
over the stone-built city
I should leave, but I can't.
Always I hear your name when I'm alone
and when I'm not alone."

Just as his letters blurred,
a burning poppy,
cut from his draggled garden
fell from the envelope
that closed
like a grave.

DIVISION

"When a child was claimed by two mothers, King Solomon said that God had created a man's vital organs in duplicate sets, so that if he were carved in two, both halves would live."

Midrash Tehillim

I might have let him hack you with a sword—
that wise King Solomon—who swore that man
has two of everything, and saved one heart,
one mind, and left the rest. She never knew
you came in pairs, and wanted you complete.

Forgive me, love. I never craved her half,
nor coveted her Syrian timpani.
Indeed, I pocketed your words of love,
uttered only when water drowns the sound.

Divided man, you have two scraggy faces,
one turned toward the sun, one to the moon.
You write to me from left to right, to her
in God's calligraphy, your country's custom,
never mingling them, for fear of babel.
Now only in dreams you speak two languages,
fluent as wind. I wake to listen
to flickering sentences, and I store half
the ashes of your dreams in a cardboard box.

Half-lives, half-selves. I, too, am split apart.
You call me by false names, guarding our doorways.
In waterfront cafés, I watch the sea,
you scan the land for some familiar faces,
until we part and shatter into halves
or break like rock into a thousand pieces.

42

IV. SEACOASTS OF THREE CONTINENTS

SEACOASTS OF THREE CONTINENTS:

1.

TROMPE L'OEIL

Right as it seemed,
it was wrong.
The cardinal tipped
a brittle stalk;
the pines were hemlocks;
through an elm's tangled leaves,
we saw the moon
split into diamond chips;
the reedy soprano
stammered Mozart's Vespers;
even the angel of fire and air
that whooshed into our room
and folded diaphanous wings
against cracked walls
was really an angel
of silence,
pleading death.

In a starless time
we walked under stars;
on an uncharted continent
we climbed mountain terraces;

on parched land
we flowed into rivulets
and heard rocks sing
in the sea wind,
and saw God's chariot throne
in a ball of fire
coming down over water.

The last light of day
reddened your face
as you boarded a plane.
You returned to a country
of rockets and explosions,
to read lists of names
enclosed in black margins,
and, for the first time,
in middle life,
to question the detonations,
cry down the guns,
remembering our peace
in a wrong world,
and try to forgive
the angel of silence
that governs our lives.

2.

APOLOGIA

When we were two beings, enclosed in separate
husks, with different cells, we palmed aside
the hour when you, a foreign guest, would leave.
"My country's torn, but mine. I must return,"

you said. How could you know our love would run
wild, in acid soil shaded from light,
across eight thousand miles? How did it happen?
It must have been a miracle, or a bed
of nails. Dazzled, we took the miracle.

Then old vows failed. We found no words
without each other's; hands, arms ripped apart,
held fast despite water, despite land;
then you told her my name you had not named,

fearing the carillon inside your chest.

3.

BURNING THE DEAD

"Although the ancients did not know the precise reasons for removing the dead from society, all civilizations have done so. In modern times, we know that infection can be spread from the dead to the living."

Another assault on Syria, the casualties
mount, your son's away, your neighbor's two
children dead in combat. Radio news:
Lebanon's dead are burned to keep the city
free from epidemics. Sounds of torches.
Cluster bombs scathe Lebanon's civilians . . .
your enemies, your friends. Once, years before,
lying on sand, you gunned armed tanks to win
a country, Israel; now you would return
most of it, but can't. Leaders want war.
You cry, "Cease fire," David mourning an Absalom
he wanted whole, say bitterly, "Peace now."
Racing to bury fallen hope, we watch
our love mount, casualties too high to reckon.

4.

BACK STREETS

No Back Streets in our time? I've known them: winding,
sinuous black grooves, and the geometry
of black-and-yellow street signs: "Dead Slow," "Danger."
I've walked the labyrinthine alleyways
and swampy paths of villages and cities;
side entrances to our cafés, gray doorways,
narrow crevices, and unlit roads.

Nor does old language fade: "mistress," "adultery,"
"secret love" are cant. Street scenes are triangles,
discovered lies, disasters. Our address,
local and permanent, is Number Seven,
our hidden marriage, visible and still
unspoken. Neighbors regard us with concern,
friends turn aside. Our faces are one face.

One sentence for that crime: walk in the light,
a man and a woman in one room, then home
to Back Street, crossing rocky paths, I leading
by several paces, you falling behind.

5.

PORT OF MANY NAMES

Three years since we met: our fire has burned,
airless, on seacoasts of three continents:
Remember Akko, Accho, Saint Jean d'Acre,
Acre, ancient port of many names?
For thousands of years, Crusaders, Arabs, Jews,
fought over it, renamed it, watched it change.

Clear as your black eyes, under Roman arches,
waves mauled the craggy rocks, fish leaped in nets,
marauders threatened to crawl in from sea.
Furtively we moved in blazing light.
Torrents of rain, dry sun. Gray sky on one
side of a tower, deep blue on the other.

Gulls reeled and soared above two tawny figures.
As flaming water under igneous sun
is water all the more, we gave our names
to one another, changing to be ourselves.
Then suddenly, we wrenched our hands apart
to stop the blood-hot current coursing through them.

6.

NOT THE ANGEL

True, you are not the angel I have molded.
Knowing we inhabited the heavens,
I wove your coat of snow; hammered your wings;
amplified your out-of-tune hosannahs.

Born into two languages, two worlds,
you fly to me, fly to your country, scrawl:
"I've lost touch with myself. It's not the war,
but my unwillingness to live without you."
Then: "I cannot leave what I have built
without destroying everything. Bear with me."
Hankering for Scotch, you reel in pain,
unfit to bring your two fixed minds together.

You are an angel, half-divine, half-man,
and heteroclitish, one of those odd thrones
who loved a woman. Joined, we are two ruined
halves of one whole angel, doomed to fall.

7.

CORRESPONDENCE

Trembling like stars that shine centuries later,
after they've moved, we utter dated vows
seaward, held back by two weeks' postal lag.

You write: "There is the paring of a moon,
one star, above the Limping Man's Café.
Patience. [One word crossed out.] We soar so high
it's any wonder we can land unharmed."

My full moon rises, and its threads are stars.
Wind tries the oak. You shaped your syllables
weeks past, to mollify my fears, your fears.

Back in your stone home, gazing at the pomegranate
tree, you see my face in Wedgwood clouds,
in the golden wall that carves your city, raging
at murderous laws you must defend, or change.

Just as we damn the day we met, we bless it.
I speak in your tones, see with your eyes
and know our love will darken

only as a tower turns black when sun
passes behind it. Now we clutch at wires,
measuring breath-lengths of our years together,
indelible as frost. That is, will be, our life.

V. INSTRUCTIONS FOR A JOURNEY

THE FLIGHT

That day I hired a private detective to follow me,
and could not read his notes. In a tangled grove,
I hid behind white pines, compressed my body,
then watched him write, left-handed and myopic,
under an Irish cap, when I asked for help
from strangers who spoke Slavic languages.
Wary, moving ahead, I found a depot,
watched an immense train churn, haloed in steam,
and boarded, second class. I had no ticket,
and my expired passport represented
a drooping head with unfamiliar eyes.
Unshaken, rows behind, the stranger waited,
wielding camera and pen. Across the border
I disembarked, but knew he would capture me,
with soundless footsteps, even on black gravel.

I tried to recall my crime. I know I am guilty,
but lose it now. Lawless, I have ignored
those signs: *"WRONG WAY: GO BACK"* and *"NO WAY OUT,"*
circles that tell me *"YOU ARE HERE."* I gather
it is the whispers that explode, the looks
that make dogs whimper. When I bow in prayer
I think of love; I know I've killed my friends,
pelting them with a touch—and yet I've heard
they are alive. Besides that's not the real

offense. I would cross any path, or trek
through swamps to find my crime. But even he,
that bald, insistent man who follows me,
unsleeping, cannot tell me what I've done.

THE MARSH

For years nothing grew
in acid soil
near my house
that stood on scant legs.
Then, year by year, I saw
sassafras and glasswort;
creepers curled around
bayberry trees,
tall stalks hunted soil
to live. Nearby, shadblow trees
with striated, gunmetal bark
lifted wiry branches.
Then fires of wind and water
burned the marsh;
only bare vines,
hooked into elms,
survived,
as we had, joined
together, in the house
on bulldozed sandy ground,
draggled, storm-blown,
still holding fast
to memories of dense grasses
and green vines
as if we knew life's law
was cleave or die.

THE SILENT VOICES

My road flows between shimmering mountains:
above, the color of calcium, gone higher
than icy clouds, and deep black gaps below us.
Our Fiat shrieks on turns, a getaway car
whose passengers, poets from China, Ghana,
haven't a syllable in common, sing
their lines to crowds in galleries and churches,
under black icons: saints wring slanted heads,
three fingers wrenched in holy benedictions.

The message read: "Please. You are ordered to leave
for Shtip, our guest, at 5 a.m. tomorrow."
No signature. Later, the dark Elena
poured wine and asked: "Better to say 'invited'?"
scanning her dictionaries.
                      "No," I said,
"Better your way. You routed me from bed."
The country is a fountain of three languages,
Serbo-Croatian, Macedonian,
Slovene. All news is good, without a word
of strikes or wars. I lift black phones that squall,
the only jarring sounds in that white silence.
"Where are your dissidents?" I asked Elena.
"There is no word for dissidents," she said,
at least none we could find in her three dictionaries.

LETTER FROM NICARAGUA

(Variations on a letter from Pablo Antonio Cuadra in July, 1979, during the rebellion against General Anastasio Somoza's leadership.)

"Querida Grace: The Lake is phosphorescent,
mirroring hills, a freshwater sea of sharks
called Cocibolca, 'lair of the great snake,'
ripples and lapses under the rickety wharf.
Ceibas wear cotton ruffs, and other trees
undulate in winds...."

        I've heard the news
and see them hauling Pedro Joaquín,
your murdered cousin, in a *via crucis*
through spattered roads. They come from fields and swamps:
hog-raisers, farmers, fishermen, makers of nets
lining the sky with lanterns, candles, fire
for the wake. Even the shells are silent.
Tomorrow, rifles will ignite sky's tinder.
The dead lie on the streets. The city's burning.

Your oracle sits mute on the Eagle's Rock,
Troy blazing, blind, fixed on the foam-capped water;
your canticles of praise gasped under thunder,
Pablo, your voice fills sails. You prod horizons,
your eyes kindling the sea, waiting for dawn.

JERUSALEM STREET TALK

Outside, the vernacular is many languages.
Syllables hide under cypresses
that screen Mount Zion;
silent cries stir the Western Wall
where letters to God
shoot up like wildflowers
that break through stone.
Copts and Ethiopians
hardly speak to one another,
and sing to separate gods.
The people's harsh voices
strike steel.

IMAGES OF GRAVITY

1.

Buoyancy:
The wind moves
a swamp reed
that the finch rides.

2.

Force:
Swallows
plummet like hail,
careening
over wild roses.

3.

Vector:
Bulrushes
gesture in wind,
dancer's arms.

4.

Density:
Gulls,
angular in flight,
stand pot-bellied.

5.

Weightlessness:
I've heard the albatross
sleeps on the wing
in the heart of a storm,
gliding
on currents it raises.

6.

Acceleration:
Dead
birds
fall
fast.

7.

Balance:
Fragile as a grasshopper,
my house stands
on spindly pilings.

8.

Momentum:
Waves crash
still rising
in vapor.

SONGS OF OUR CELLS

In dreams I hear the songs I cannot hear:
leeches tap, earthworms and snakes
rattle their skeletons.
                                    In these white pines
the thrush, the red-winged blackbird and the dove
sing in antiphony; under that earthly clatter,
I hear a canorous thunder and I know
I am inhabited by tiny remnants—
bits of viruses and organelles—
that go through evolutionary storms
with genes of fathers. Carrying the dead,
we are descended from a single cell,
waking to song.

FIRE IN THE LAKE

It must have been a forest
that blazed, then flooded.
Pines stand gaunt; charred
upturned branches kindle
visions of green starbursts
until the mind casts
capsized images
of pine needles
in black opal water
stitched with sun's
threads. Burned water
is water all the more.

THE ISLAND

So slender
is the island
that I can see sun ignite the bay
and strike the ocean
at the same time.
Larks sweep the sky
soon to be scarlet;
beyond shadblow trees
presumptuous catbrier climbs
a pine tree, and tall stalks
sway like metronomes,
displacing patens,
claiming the marshland.

Here I find it strange
to find peace strange.
The island
is no more real
than the moon's singularity;
it will change
as a cloud's shape
alters in wind,
as storms move dunes
and sea-spray crops
their heather.

Surely as the ocean batters
the sand's composure
prodding the shoreline inland,
this land will change
just as the boat develops out of fog
and courses through water
to carry me
from my house
on stilts in sand.

DAWN OVER THE EAST RIVER

Perhaps it is a new beginning after all.
The sun that ignites the bridge will fire
bricks and glass, while remnants of stars
fade like your arms remembered.
My face in the slate-gray river is my face,
not yours, nor any angel in the wind
my other self. I am my form, my name.

Still on this bank your voice pierces the mist
sun burns from earth (it has rained for days):
my night-blind heart rises like steam
from plane trees trawling shadows,
breaking into bud in the slant light.
Here everything floats skyward: gulls rise,
smoke lifts from tugboats, twists from chimneys.
Wind thrashes cellophane, unloosing litter.

Before the sun's red eye is visible
it lights black clouds and shapes
formless buildings. It marries earth,
reinventing incandescent questions.

SMALL METEOR

As comets go, it was a disappointment.
However perilously close to earth
it circled, still it wreaked no tidal waves,
fired no earthquakes, demons or disasters.
Astronomers predicted blazing flight,
then blinked at its arrival. You could hardly
see it in darkness, let alone by day,
before it dwindled. Only the tireless few
saw it after sundown, with binoculars.

Still, that shooting star, thrust into space,
recalled that rock may burn suddenly, spin
for centuries before it shines, and rise
falling, surviving night.
                  I told my friend
about the paltry star, and he shook loose
from memory the comet of 1910,
screened through smoked glass. When I saw his eyes
go gray I knew how anything alive
may flare, shine and survive. Small star: small miracle.

INSTRUCTIONS FOR A JOURNEY

"God commanded Metatron, the Angel of the Face, to conduct Moses to the celestial regions amid the sound of music and song."
Gedullet Mosheh

There are no provisions, but your guide
may teach you hymns during the long flight.
Sing lauds and benedictions on all nights
to soothe the guards of houses, one inside

the other. Take your journal, and a pen,
staplers and dictionaries, when you travel.
The landscape may appear unusual:
gray birds sail low; birches are frozen bones.

Prepare to see men seventy miles high,
their shoulders parasangs apart, with many heads
and tongues. All measurements are odd. Their eyes
flash lightning. Then the terror, as your body

assumes new forms, abandoning old molds.
First Heaven: Go through "Customs" and "Security."
You'll see blunt hills the color of chalcedony.
Igneous water flows in riverbeds.

Chapels have stained-glass windows cut in moonstone,
marked "war" and "peace." Angels who pacify
the world praise God; they are condemned to die
if they sing louder than men, or out of tune.

In Sixth Heaven, angels of wrath and silence
greet you. Cherubs and seraphim dance;
gazelles with dappled faces bear the throne;
light strikes the trembling heart. You are alone.

You'll see a God of fire trailing stars,
climb ladders, see the chariot throne, and still
survive unharmed. Through blinding flame, through water,
you enter seven heavens and fall, whole.

About the author

Grace Schulman has published a book of poems, *Burn Down the Icons* (Princeton University Press, 1976). She translated T. Carmi's *At the Stone of Losses* (Jewish Publication Society and The University of California Press, 1983; Carcanet Press, London, 1983, edited *Ezra Pound: A Collection of Criticism* (McGraw-Hill, 1974), and co-translated *Songs of Cifar and the Sweet Sea* by Pablo Antonio Cuadra (Columbia University Press, 1979). Her study, *Marianne Moore: The Poetry of Engagement,* is forthcoming from The University of Illinois Press.

She has been Poetry Editor of *The Nation* since May, 1972, and from January, 1974 through June, 1984 was Director of the Poetry Center at the 92nd Street YM-YWHA. She is a professor of English at Baruch College in New York, and holds a Ph.D. from New York University.